A Man Without A Voice

A Man Without A Voice

A Photographer's Nightmare

******A book every photographer should read*******

R. Sterling

This book is the product of a true experience and is the reflection of the thoughts, and expressions of the people interviewed with respect to the law, and the Constitution of the United States.

This book was printed in the United States of America.

To order additional copies of this book, contact:
Xlibris Corporation
1-888-795-4274
www.Xlibris.com
Orders@Xlibris.com
73721

Acknowledgements

I would like to thank all the inmates, and people that participated in the interviews, and submitting their experiences in this matter. Hopefully in getting this information out to the public we will be able to get some of these issues, and concerns reviewed and ultimately changed. Our judicial system is heading the wrong way in handling our inmates. I hope to make people realize in some cases it's not the inmate that's at fault it's the court system letting them down.

In this wonderful world we live in wouldn't it be nice if all the people of the earth would follow Jesus' teachings of "Love thy neighbour as thy self, and be merciful just and pure."

Everybody has the ability of forgiving others for what they may or may not have done. It's not up to anyone of us in this material world to judge any other person, then commit them to any kind of sentencing. If you remember it was a lie told to the people that relied on human emotion to convince the judge that committed Jesus to death. But the most important action is for you to forgive yourself.

Short Summary

I took up photography about 20 years ago. I bought my first 35 mm SLR camera. Didn't know too much about SLR cameras at that time so I took a basic photography course at the local Jr College.

I got started shooting landscapes, and still photography. I was told by my photography instructor that I had a knack for the art. I started photographing friends, and shooting family portraits, as well as sporting events etc. I would photograph anything just to get the experience.

When I started taking photos of people I developed a real love for the art. People are very interesting subjects, and no two are the same. It gives a photographer a real challenge with lighting, aperture settings, and exposure. You also have the ability to do special effects with lighting, and props, clothing etc.

About three years ago I was contacted by a person that designed costumes, and other clothing for the stage. She wanted to use her daughter for the model, and have catalogues made with the different designs.

This lady also wanted her daughter to get into the movie industry, and wanted me to sponsor her. If she was selected for a job, that sponsorship would include all her photos, comp cards, advertising, and most of all travel. Her daughter at that time was under the age of eighteen, and considered a minor. I told her, that she was her mother, and responsible for her own daughter, and signing of contracts, negotiating deals etc. I could not represent her. So I put her in contact with several booking agents in the area, but they wanted about $500 for this. The mom told me they wanted too much money, and wanted me to pay her fee. I told her it was her responsibility not mine. She got mad, and said I paid for one other person, and why not her daughter. I explained to her that the girl in question was my daughter. She got very upset with me!

About three years after that I got a phone call from a detective at the local sheriffs department saying that this lady had filed a complaint against me saying that I molested her daughter. I told the detective that the mother was with us every time I took photos of her daughter. Since she was there she knew nothing happened. I also told the detective that the mother has every picture I ever took of her daughter. As a mater of fact this mother told the detective on a tape recorded interview that, and I quote "I know you didn't have sex with her daughter" end of quote. So you would think that would be the end of it . . . . But no not in this county. When I contacted an attorney he said it sounded to him like an extortion charge. The mother trying to get some kind of financial settlement. That's fairly common anymore. It seems to be a quick way for some people to get money. What they don't understand is that it destroys a family for ever! But as you know these kind of people don't care about you and me they just care about themselves, and how they look to other people.

I found out that guilty or not guilty they go ahead with the accusations to see what happens. In my case they delayed it for well over a year or so, almost until the they exceeded the statute of limitations, and would have had to dismissed the charges.

Prologue

While you read through this book I would like you to know that I have the utmost respect for the laws of our land. I think our court system is the best in the world. We have the Constitution of the United States for a guideline in the performance of these laws. The Constitution of the United States was written to protect you and me, and to see that every citizen has an equal opportunity, and to be free. That's' our God given right. But we have to be cautious because there are many people that want to take that right away from us.

None of us are perfect in this world of ours that's why we are here. We all need to gain knowledge to make us better people, and this world a better place to live. However, once in a while people stumble or trip on this road of life, and do something that they wish they didn't. It doesn't mean they are bad people. Everybody does it, including you. None of us are perfect. People are intelligent, and most of them know what they did, and know it's wrong. Unfortunately our judicial system causes severe punishment even for a little stumble. If they would meet this with a little understanding, and consideration this would be a much better world then it is now. But you always have the radicals that believe the world would be a better place without the people that make mistakes. They just don't realize they are making a huge mistake themselves. These people are generally the ones that cause the majority of the problems for everybody. There are many different laws that keep us all in line with everybody else, and when you accidentally cross over that line, our governing body called law enforcement swings into action. This is a good thing.

The problem: Our laws are written with many loopholes, and many ways of interpreting them. They are not cut and dried. It's how the governing body understands any particular law, and how it applies to whatever case they are working on. Human emotion and public opinion plays a very big part in how a judge handles a case. It shouldn't, but it does. You have to understand our laws are written by lawyers for lawyers, and you and I don't stand a chance. That's why we need lawyers to represent us in a court of law just because we who are not lawyers, don't understand the wording they use. It is very confusing, and it is meant to be that way. Our laws are written so they can be interpreted in many different ways or to comply with any situation based on how the individual understands it. The law is left open so the person in charge can interpret it any way they want to meet the requirements needed, or can be interpreted by human emotion, and still be in compliance. Someone said a long time ago where there is confusion there is profit, or in the court system there is conviction. In a lot of cases it is the understanding of the law by a specific individual that convicts the person, and not the way the law was written or intended to be enforced. Sometimes the person doesn't have to commit any crime to be considered guilty. That is bad enough, but when it comes to sex cases, now you have the human element, and emotion to deal with, and the law goes out the window for all practical purposes. Our court system and judges allow the human emotion to influence the outcome of these cases. If the law enforcement person doesn't have any evidence to prosecute a person the court allows ample time to create the evidence they need. In my experience the court allowed the investigating person to violate the law in order to create evidence which they did, and even while doing that they violated the ordinance that provided the ability to do this. So they broke the law not only once but twice. The court said that was OK. So what it boils down to is this. The court ended up violating the law on two occasions to create circumstantial evidence to convict this person of something he didn't do.

It is generally known that sometimes the only way to get evidence that someone has broken the law is to break the law yourself to obtain the information illegally. The idea is to find a judge that will issue an order to break the law, and because he is the one that determines who goes to jail or not, guess what? You Lose! Again!

Ninety nine percent of all law enforcement people are just trying to do a good job under a lot of pressure, and they need to be commended for that. In the area where I live our local Sheriff's Department are mostly good people but it's the few in this department that make it bad for everybody. Most of the people in our county have no respect for our Sheriff's Department at all, and that includes the local police departments.

I took up photography about 20 years ago. I bought my first 35 mm SLR camera. Didn't know too much about SLR cameras at that time so I took a basic photography course at the local Jr College.

I got started shooting landscapes, and still photography. I was told by my photography instructor that I had a knack for the art. I started photographing friends, and shooting family portraits, as well as sporting events etc. I would photograph anything just to get the experience.

When I started taking photos of people I developed a real love for the art. People are very interesting subjects, and no two are the same. It gives a photographer a real challenge with lighting, aperture settings, and exposure. You also have the ability to do special effects with lighting, and props, clothing etc.

About three years ago I was contacted by a person that designed costumes, and other clothing for the stage. She wanted to use her daughter for the model, and have catalogues made with the different designs.

This lady also wanted her daughter to get into the movie industry, and wanted me to sponsor her. That sponsorship would include all her photos, comp cards, advertising, and most of all travel. Her daughter at that time was under the age of eighteen, and considered a minor. I told her, that she was her mother. and responsible for her daughter, and signing contracts, negotiating deals etc. if she was selected for a job. I could not represent her. So I put her in contact with several booking agents in the area, but they wanted about $500 for comp card and advertising. The mom told me they wanted too much money, and wanted me to pay her fee. I told her it was her responsibility, not mine. She got mad, and said I paid for one other person and why not her daughter. I explained to her that the girl in question was my daughter. She got very upset with me!

About three years after that I got a phone call from a detective at the local sheriffs department saying that this lady had filed a complaint against me saying that I molested her daughter. I told the detective that the mother was with us every time I took photos of her daughter. Since she was there she knew nothing happened. I also told the detective that the mother has every picture I ever took of her daughter. As a mater of fact this mother told the detective on a tape recorded interview that, and I quote "I know you didn't have sex with my daughter" end of quote. So you would think that would be the end of it . . . . But no, not in this county. When I contacted an attorney he said it sounded to him like an extortion charge. The mother trying to get some kind of financial settlement. That's fairly common today. It seems to be a quick way for some people to get money. What they don't understand is that it destroys a family forever! But as you know these kind of people don't care about you and me they just care about themselves, and how they look to other people.

I found out that guilty, or not guilty, they go ahead with the accusations to see what happens. In my case they delayed it for over a year or so, almost until the they exceeded the statute of limitations, and would have had to dismiss the charges.

Photographers beware!

His book is written not to gain any money, or fame, but to try and alert photographers, and the general public about what is happening in our law enforcement community, and judicial districts in relation to photographers, and their duties and responsibilities to their client. Our law enforcement, and judicial areas are very judgemental, and I found that in my state a person is automatically assumed guilty until proven he or she is innocent. Especially photographers. When it comes to posing, adjusting clothing, brushing hair and, anything else that deals with touching a female client during the process of taking the best photo possible.

Model agents want a specific format. The theatre director wants something different, and the movie industry wants still another format. It is almost impossible for a photographer not to touch the client during the course of the photo shoot. Then on top of all that you have these goody two shoes that think they know everything there is to know, and how they think it should be done, but they don't have a clue how to get there. These people just think it happens! These people think that all the pictures they see in magazines, catalogues, and other advertisements just happen. Well you and I both know it takes a lot of work to make a photo look great. It just doesn't happen! These people are the ones a photographer has to watch out for. They are dangerous. Be very careful.

All of the information in this book is gathered by my personal experience as a photographer and other photographers who have dealt with the court system, attorneys, and law enforcement agencies. Because of the corruption and dishonesty in this county's' judicial system and law enforcement, specifically the local sheriff's department, it allowed me to get an inside look at how they do business, and treat the inmates assigned to their care. They are so judgmental about everything about every activity in the jail system. I am trying to get this information out in hopes that all photographers, and the general public can be made aware, and be watchful of the pitfalls in our judicial community with respect to the art of photography. It is my intent to inform all photographers, and make them aware of how law enforcement looks at how you do your job. Please remember, if you touch a female at any time she can accuse you of assaulting her. If she wants to make a big enough deal about it you could end up in jail. If you take photos of high school seniors, model portfolios, or any other photos that involve a female subject. Beware.

Chapter 1

Even if you, the photographer have the best intentions for your client, she can turn it around in a heartbeat, and make you sound like Jack the Ripper.

Even if the female is lying, law enforcement, could think that there is something to the girl's story, and they will arrest you anyway just on suspicion of a sexual assault.

Then the news media gets wind of the story, and you might as well hang up your equipment, because you are out of business! Once the general public hears about these things they go berserk, and want revenge on you because now you are known as a sleaze ball, or a pervert that can't be trusted. Then it gets worse from there.

Sometimes even if you have a second person as a witness be very careful. Be sure you take the name of the witness, and relationship to the client. You also need to record the time the client arrives at your studio, and the time they leave. Then you have to make a decision about whether or not to trust the second person or not. If you have bad feelings, get out of that situation as fast as you can, and don't let the door smack you in the ass on the way out! In my case I had the girl's mother with us, and she witnessed the photo session. I didn't even think about not trusting the mother. But I should have!

The girls mother was the one that filed the report with the local sheriff's department. Go figure?

The general public does not understand a photographer's job, and duties in getting the best pictures possible.

As every photographer knows it is sometimes necessary for a photographer to actually touch the person being photographed during the posing, and picture taking process. Then you have to adjust clothing, get wrinkles out of the clothing, brushing hair etc.

During this time the average person may misunderstand this process, and may think you are trying to do something your are not supposed to be doing. Be aware if you get a nut case with a chip on her shoulder—Look Out! Or one that is trying to get some money from you in any way they can.

I need to talk about another very important item that a photographer should never overlook. That's the model release and property release form. Very Important! As a photographer you sell photos to different agencies. If that agency publishes your photo, and someone can identify themselves in it they are entitled to payment. However, if you have a signed model and property release on file, they through the release, are granting your their permission to publish, and license their photos as you see fit. Don't overlook this process. There are many of these releases forms on the internet.

My whole case was based on a three year old, fifth generation story that was told to a mother by one of her neighbours that was told to her by her daughter that heard it from her daughters friend, and so on. This story bounced around back and forth between several teenage girls and their friends for at least three years before it was reported to the mother, and then to the authorities. By that time it was so totally changed, and out of whack you wouldn't believe it. But you should! These people took something simple and innocent, and changed it to something ugly, devastating, and not true, and just a plain bold faced lie.

Remember it is easier and quicker for people to believe a lie then it is to believe the truth. That's just human nature. One cannot take energy from another person to build themselves up without paying a price later on in their life.

It seems that people, like the mother in this instance, is after their fifteen minutes of fame to build themselves up at the expense of other people's feelings. As you know, if you have a circle of twenty or more people, and you tell a simple story to the first one, and tell him to pass it on, by the time it gets to the last person then back, to you, the story is completely different. That's because everybody hears it differently, or likes to add their own twist to make it more interesting, or both. This mother added her two bits based on what she has seen on TV, read in novels, and read in the newspapers then told her twisted story to the news media, about what she thinks may of happened, and you know how the news media thinks! If a story isn't bad enough to sell their papers they add their two cents to it, and change it around to make it more juicy, exciting, and so on. You know the saying about the news media "If it bleeds it leads and they "specialize in bad news. Everybody will watch a plane crash with blood and guts, but how many people will watch scouts selling cookies at the grocery store. The media knows this, and media outlets are profit corporations. They offer what sells, and when criticized, they try to defend their actions by "justifying" them in one way or another. A story gets out of hand real quick. So by the time this story was reported to the local law enforcement, news media and TV station it was a completely twisted lie, it made me into somebody I couldn't possibly be.

It is totally against my nature and up bringing to hurt any child, let alone take advantage of one. But because there was so much said, and this person made it sound so bad everybody that heard it pictured in their own mind what must of happened. based on their own exposure to TV, novels, and again the news media.

Chapter 2

It was very hard for people, and law enforcement, to find the truth. It's like the difference between night and day. I was never allowed to give my side of the story. The judge would not allow any evidence in my behalf. The court would say that I, my wife, children, and co-workers could make up stories and lie to try and prove my innocence. So they acted on human feelings, public opinion, and fear instead of hard factual evidence, or any material facts that would indicate that a crime was ever committed. This process proceeded without any evidence or facts to support what they charged me with. Special note: There were no facts or evidence to support any crime having being committed, let alone committed by me.

I was never alone with the alleged complainant. I was told by my attorney that the young lady at one time said that I never did the things her mother said I did. They told the young lady she was a minor, and was not allowed to say anything or testify in this case. It was all her mother doing the accusing. At one time the prosecuting attorney told my attorney that he believed the mother was, and I quote **"a nut case!"**

Now, because my work requires me to write an accurate daily resume as to what happens every day, I could account for almost every minute of every day during the time this alleged crime supposedly took place. I recorded times on and off the jobs, phone numbers of people I talked to, where I was, and all the times, and locations of the meetings I had to attend and much more. The point is, I could account for every minute of my time. So the question is. When did this happen? The mother couldn't pick a time.

The mother said she didn't know when it took place it just happened. Well, we all know things just don't happen. There has to be a time, place, and the opportunity. The mother couldn't pick a time where it would be possible because all my time was accounted for with the help of the resume.

I found out during this experience that in any kind of sexual assault cases, especially if the girl is under the age of 18, the parent has the luxury of being able to choose any time he or she wants within a 365 day period of time. Even if it isn't the actual date and time the alleged crime was supposed to have happened. The court allows this because they figure that any child under the age of 18 is not legally responsible for their own actions and, has a very short memory with this kind of situation.

So they started asking me when I thought it could of happened? Again this is an example of them trying to twist things around trying to get you to admit something. Be careful how you answer. If you don't understand or are not sure of the question you need to ask them to rephrase the question until it's clear what they want. Then only answer the question, and that's all. Do not elaborate on anything.

Chapter 3

If you are a photographer reading this book, please keep a resume' of all your actions with your clients, times, and locations. And always, always have a second person present when photographing females. They can turn on you in a heart beat, and if you don't have any record you will have no chance of defending yourself. In my case I did have someone there, and it still didn't help. It is possible, if you get a honest judge, maybe the court will give you the opportunity to defend your actions, and present your evidence to clear yourself. But, in this day and age, I think it would be hard to find a court that would really listen to your side of the story, and let you present evidence to back it up.

Everybody has their own agenda, and claim they have a short budget so it's just in, and out as quick as possible. Law enforcement says they don't have enough money to actually investigate any case. They just cannot take the time to investigate everything.

Everything is politics now days. Our court system in this state has a lot of judges that perform very poorly. They have a system, but it's their system, and they run it. It is hard to fight their system, especially when they are the system, and in charge, and they make up the rules, and regulations in their system. They are the boss, and there is nobody to challenge their actions except the public.

You could say, why don't you file a complaint with the State District Attorney? But you have to realize they to are part of the system as well. The public needs to go to their state representative, and demand some changes be made in these matters. Remember these representatives are working for us. At least that's the way it's suppose to be. They need to make sure that law enforcement investigates any alleged crime completely before proceeding. Quote "Do it right the first time, because you may never have a second chance!" In these cases they need to do it right the first time or a family gets destroyed.

When something like this hits the news media the general public forms thoughts, and opinions in their own mind of what they think took place based on the news media story, stories they have read, what they've seen on TV, and novels they have read, and not the truth. By this time nobody knows the truth! If there were any evidence it would be contaminated.

The news media controls the public opinion, and actions based on what they report, and how they report it. Everybody's thinking is affected in some way by what they read, and when the news media comes up with some of these stories it's hard to ignore them.

Chapter 4

BE CAREFUL—WATCH YOUR BACK!
Example—Think about it!

The author describes the ocean as being calm, and the waves gently unfolding on the warm sand with palm trees all around, and you setting there reading a good book, and deep in thought. You look up, and see a very beautiful young lady walking across in front of you. As you admire her you notice she is wearing a French bikini with little flowers on it, and it barely covers her. Your imagination runs wild, and you see you and her in a wonderful and loving relationship. Just then she sits down next to you, and everything is quiet. You look up and see a sail boat quietly sailing in the peaceful distance, and the warm breeze blowing gently across your face. You imagine yourself on that sailboat with the young lady of your dreams when she walks up to you and says . . . .

If you pictured that scene in your thought, I have successfully controlled your thinking for at least a couple of seconds. That is the power of thought, and that is what the news media is doing every day to its readers whether it is about crime, government, or political issues. They are guilty of placing thoughts in peoples minds, and therefore controlling there outcome. That's why is so important that you base your results on facts, and evidence that cannot be changed, and not on what somebody says about someone else. You need to rely on facts that cannot be changed, and not on human emotion.

Even if they record an interview with you just remember that all the tapes can be altered with any computer. By taking a frequency sample they can make you say anything they want, and call it evidence. Now days it seems that all computers have that capability, and can alter anything electronically. Even though the law does not allow this type of evidence to be submitted to the court it depends on the judge hearing the case.

The judge can sign an order to allow the law to be broken in special cases to accommodate their goal whatever that might be. Even though they don't have any evidence they can create some given enough time. Just look back at history. How many people do you know or have heard about that went to jail or prison by mistake. Just recently they let a man out of prison after fifteen years who was convicted of child rape, only to find out that the girl lied about the crime. That person sat in prison for fifteen years, lost all his family, his wife, home, job and everything he owns because of a lie that law enforcement believed was true. This girl with the help of a very judgemental law enforcement system, and the courts being very corrupt, and not relying on hard and factual evidence put this innocent person in prison, and ruined his life. And the kicker is when they let the man out of prison they just said sorry. Now how does that make you feel?

Suppose this was one of your family members. Could you handle it? We need to do something about this kind of activity, and get your congressman to change or at least look into these matters of injustice. Let's get these laws changed, or at least amended. It may be you next time!

That's why it's very important to have physical evidence especially in these types of cases where the judge has a personal interest, or takes a person's recorded testimony as the only evidence. When the judge does something like that, the accusing person can say anything they want, and the judge will believe them. In my case the prosecuting attorney made the statement to my attorney saying, and I quote **"my client is a nut case!"** No matter how out of whack a person's thinking is, the judge will hear them, and make judgment on what they are saying because they base their judgment on human emotion and not fact. And please remember once a person has said something it can never be taken back!

Chapter 5

In the report, the mother accused me of having sex with her under aged daughter. However in a recorded phone tap interview with the sheriff's department detective, she specifically stated when talking to me, and I quote *"I know you didn't have sex with my daughter"* unquote. So I ask you why did they proceed with the investigation and try to convict me for something I didn't do? Here the girls mother stated on the tape that she knows I didn't have sex with her daughter! Why didn't law enforcement believe her when she said that? Again I think it's because people in general like to rub their noses in smut, and garbage! It gives them some kind of enjoyment to hear about somebody else's problems, and glad it is not theirs.

I was never given my rights! I was never arrested, and at no time ever even to this day has the Sheriff's department set foot on my property for anything concerning this case. They didn't even try to find out about the case or even look for any evidence. You know why . . . . That is because there was no crime, and I think they knew that, but they needed time to create evidence to try and convict me to make themselves look good. By this time law enforcement was so deep into this with the news media following every step they made, they wouldn't dare say "ooops" we made a mistake! This will never ever happen with our elected officials! They are always pointing their finger at someone else to take the blame, and then taking the credit for themselves.

The best thing a person can do is not say anything about anything. Just be quiet simply because everything you say they somehow will turn it against you in some way, or another.

Take Note: Have you ever heard of a deaf mute person being convicted, and taken to jail for any crime?

Chapter 6

You, dear reader think about this . . . . The accusations started out as seven felony charges with a 20 year prison sentence. A year, and some months later it ended up being an assault with sexual motivation charge with a three month sentence that was reduced to two months, and I ended up serving only one month in confinement. You know, I still don't know what happened or how. The only thing I do know is our judicial system is extremely unjust, confused, and they really don't take the time to investigate the situation. They rely on other people to do the investigation, and report to them on what they found. Some of the court mail is handled by the work release inmates from the jail. And that is a fact!

Given enough time they can create evidence out of nothing. In my case the prosecuting attorney wasn't interested in what's right or wrong, or justice, he was more interested in how he looked to the news media, and his peers. I spent over a year in, and out of the courts, and it's hard for me to believe that there is so much dishonesty involved in our professional law enforcement people. It's like when several attorneys get together in the court its like the good ol' boys club.

The judge would address a specific case but, all the attorneys in the court room would have their own conversations going on, and they were not discussing court business. We, as citizens, rely on these people for our protection, but I, and many other people are learning that the sheriff's department, court system, and the attorneys cannot be trusted in this county, or any other for that mater. In this county you are guilty until you can prove yourself innocent that is if the courts allow you to present the evidence to support your innocence.

In my case my attorney had at least 32 pages of precedence pertaining to this case, several codes and laws, that were violated and broken by the sheriff's department, and my Constitutional rights being violated. I had no voice in this case and my attorney had no voice as well. The court just did what they wanted, and ignored everything else. It's like the court system is king, and nobody can do anything or say anything unless its court approved, and they only approve what they want.

When the information was presented to the judge that would prove my innocence she didn't even read the brief. She just turned to the prosecuting attorney and asked "are we still OK" and the prosecuting attorney said "I think so" (He Thinks SO!) and at that time the judge said she would not allow the information to be entered as evidence in my behalf. My attorney was so mad he was just shaking, and red in the face. He himself couldn't believe what the judge just did, and said. How could she disallow all this factual evidence. We found out later that she was a fairly new judge, and if she allowed the evidence to be entered, the case would have been dismissed for lack of evidence on the prosecutor's part and prove that a crime was never committed.

If she would have allowed the evidence, she would have gone against the other two long-time judges that signed an order to violate the law as it is written for phone tapping. What they did was illegal, and wrong, but because the judge said it was OK the sheriff's department proceeded to break the law, and call it evidence even though by all rights it was in violation of the code. The sheriff's department didn't even follow these rules of recording the phone tap. It was all done illegally. This allowed the sheriff's department, and the court to create their own evidence to support their ideas about the case.

Chapter 7

Please don't get me wrong, our court system is the best I have ever seen, and it is set up the right way to give everybody a fair chance. However I have some serious doubts about the people that run the system. In my case I was before at least seven different judges through the year, and in every instance the judge had no knowledge of my case. He would always ask the prosecutor if he felt that the case was going OK, and the prosecutor would responded at all times and I quote: "I believe so". But he isn't sure!

In relation to the judges many people think that a judge sometimes gets burned out. They see these cases so much that they become callous in their feelings both for the person involved, and their families. They receive input from different agencies that think they are saving the world by sending this person to jail. Doesn't make any difference whether he is guilty or not, they just want to look good to the public and their friends. Once a story is told whether it is a lie or not, people tend to believe it. Again I will say, "it is easier for a person to believe a lie then it is to believe the truth. Judges should sit on the bench for a limited period of time, and not for life. They get numb in their feelings, and allow their human emotions to interfere with their decisions.

My case sat on the prosecutor's desk for two months before he decided to go ahead with it. I learned after, that if this case was in any other county it would never have gone to trial simply because there was no evidence a crime was even committed. But like I said earlier when you see, and picture something in your mind it's hard to reverse it. This was hard for the mother because she had already gone to the news media, and her story was already in the local newspaper, and then she called the local television station, and allowed them to come to her home for an interview. So she couldn't stop now without being embarrassed, and shamed by her friends. The mother made such a big deal of it, it was hard for her to back down, but she thought it was OK to ruin my life and my family that I love.

Chapter 8

One of the major things in my case that doesn't make sense is when the prosecuting attorney decided to go ahead with the case and file charges, it took him a couple of months to do so. When he finally decided to go forward with the case the prosecuting attorney charged me with seven counts of a felony. I was indicted, and appeared before a judge to plead guilty, or not guilty. I pleaded not guilty! In almost all cases of this kind when a complaint is made, the local law enforcement will come out and arrest you, read you your rights, and put you in jail until you can go before the judge and plead your case. In my case that never happened.

The charge was made, and a representative from the local sheriff's department called me on the phone, and said they had a complaint from the mother that I molested her daughter. And that was it. To this day not one person from law enforcement took any statement from me as to my side of the story. I was not arrested, or read my rights. No law enforcement came to my home to search, or inspect my computer, as is customary in these kind of cases. Not once did I have the opportunity to give my side of the story. I was always told to keep quiet, and not say anything.

After being indicted, the judge asked me how do I plead, and I said I was innocent, and not guilty. He said he would record my statement. He also said I was free to go without bail, and on my own recognizance. Now that is unheard of in cases like this. Now that I look back on it, I believe the prosecuting attorney, and the judge knew I was not guilty. But because the mother had called the news papers, and the TV station, they couldn't back down now. The media did a very good job of smearing the information, and creating their own story, and convicting me in their article and report. It would be impossible for me or anyone else to get a fair shake at a trial in this area.

This started a yearlong escapade with the county court system, and how they operate. In every case where I had to appear in court for an omnibus hearing or just a hearing to extend the trial period because the sheriff's office was not ready, the judge didn't have any history of my case. The judge would always ask the prosecuting attorney how things were progressing, and every time they said they were not ready for various reasons, and asked for a continuance. However, we were always ready, but the prosecutor was not, and always postponed the trial date. He did it so much that finally at one of the omnibus hearings he again delayed the trial, but the historian told the judge we were getting close to the statutory date for dismissal without cause. So they decided to proceed ready or not. Still no real evidence.

I found out while preparing for trial the prosecuting attorney was talking to the mother about the proceedings, and what could happen if she lost. That is we could come back on her with a case of our own. It is my understanding at that time the mother told the prosecuting attorney that quote "maybe he didn't do all that" Surprise! The prosecuting attorney, and the mother decided to present a plea bargain. To reduce all the felony charges to an assault charge, with sexual motivation. The mother agreed with the prosecuting attorney. They presented the plea bargain to my attorney, and I was advised to take it because I would never get a fair trial in this county. At the time, I thought I was agreeing to a misdemeanour or a gross misdemeanour at best. That's what I was told! About 5 minutes before I went before the judge my attorney told me that it had been changed to a class C felony. All this happened 5 minutes before seeing the judge, you have to wonder just what it was that made it change? There was no time to discuss what this meant. At the time I had no idea what was to come.

Chapter 9

GUEST OF THE COUNTY
All expenses paid. heh! Not a chance!

During the sentencing hearing the judge asked if anyone wanted to get up and add their comments in the case. It wouldn't do any good, but at least it would give these people some way to vent their opinion and anger at the proceedings thus far, and reflect the hatred of the system the way it is. One person got up, and was very violent about the way the system doesn't work, and finally the judge told him he would have to contact his congressmen if he wanted to see any change.

Of course the mother got up and wanted to add her two cents to the effort. She violently complained about the plea bargain agreement that was made saying she was disgusted with the whole idea. The reality is she was the one that came up with the idea in the first place. Every single thought, and idea has come from her in one form of another, then usually changed later on. She is the one that filed the false report, and kept the lie going by telling her friends about how the case was going, and of course adding her digs, and comments to make is sound as bad as she could. She makes herself sound like a queen, and me the devil when it is the other way around.

In fact, the prosecuting attorney told my attorney that he thought she was a "nut case" and needed to be evaluated before any trial.

In telling her friends, they added their thoughts to the story, and changed it around the way they thought it should be, and wanted to hear it. So now we have several stories going different directions, and all bad, but different.

This person always talked about how she was raped several time, and the daughter in question was the result of these rapes. She has always told her daughter that she was a result of rape, and an unwanted child. She told her daughter several times and in my presence that she was an unwanted child, and if she didn't do what her mother asked her to do she would disown her and turn her over to the courts to deal with.

So as a result her daughter lived in fear all the time, and did whatever her mother told her to do. Even to lie for her mother. Boy what a way to raise your child.

Chapter 10

The people in charge of our court system are not the greatest people to deal with in accusations like this. If you are accused of a sex crime like this you are automatically guilty until you can prove otherwise, and even then its hard to get back to normal. Remember once you or somebody else has said something you or they can never take it back. Once its out, and people form a picture in their mind, it is very hard to change the thought. So remember to think before you say something about somebody. You can do a lot of damage to yourself, and to other people, if you're not careful.

If you, as a photographer, ever get into a situation like this or something that even resembles something like this don't say anything if you can help it. Remember, the least said is the easiest mended! The court system likes to turn everything around to suit themselves and not you. If possible they will change your story around to fit whatever charges they want. You need to remember they are under the eye of the news media, and whatever the news media reports the public believes. The law enforcement people, and people that are supposed to investigate these cases make up their own rules, and are good at creating evidence to hang you from the yard arm so to speak.

Next up was a person who gave his opinion of the case and me. The judge asked him to identify himself, and he said he was the biological father to the young lady in question. Now think about this. Here is a mother that says she was raped several times by this same guy, and we have her daughter as the proof of what the mother says, and this person gets up and gives his testimony of being the biological father . . . . now wouldn't you think the judge could put two and two together and figure this out. Guess what! not a chance!! We have a man that admits that the girl is his biological daughter we have a woman that accused this man of raping her repeatedly, and we have the girl that represents the physical evidence.

Mr Watson, did I miss staff meeting or something?

He was complaining about the short sentence. The judge finally told him that if he didn't like the way the laws are written to write his congressman to see if they can change it. Even though this information was out there the judge made no comment about the crime this person had committed. How's that for our tax dollars at work? Makes you want to pay more taxes so we can have more stupid people running our government, and spending your money. On top of all that, the mother stated that she has sent her daughter to her father for a couple of week during the summer, and at that time the father molested her causing her to seek psychiatric counselling. All this long before I met her.

My wife also got the chance to speak. She spent about 15 minutes counteracting the accusations from the prosecuting attorney, the department of corrections, and the mother. Didn't seem to make any difference to the court or the prosecutor. It was hard to get anybody to believe in the truth. This lady also told the judge that she thought I molested my own daughters, and in a later letter to the court, she wrote she seemed to think I molested the whole entire senior class at the local high school. The general public, and people in general just don't want to believe in the truth, and are very easily swayed.

It was very obvious that this women was trying to make this story sound as bad as she could using anything she could get a hold of. It has always been easier to believe a lie then to believe the truth. I have always been told, and it is also in the bible where it says "If somebody accuses somebody of a crime they are generally guilty of the same crime themselves" and that is the way it works.

The Department of Corrections (DOC) also submitted a false letter to the court regarding my position. My wife and I went through 3 hours of interviews for the Pre Trial Investigation. When the letter was submitted we were mis-quoted many times, and because of that, it made me look guilty when in fact it should have been the other way around. Again DOC just does what they want with no supervision or recourse on our behalf. When I told my attorney he just looked the other way. We even sent a letter outlining all the mistakes in their letter, and made many corrections. Our attorney did nothing, figuring that a change would not be made. Like I said earlier all the attorneys are officers of the court, and they don't want to create waves. Again you are screwed!

After everybody had their chance at making me look bad I had my turn, but I was told not to say anything. I had to keep quiet. My attorney said I couldn't say anything about the case, or about the mother or her actions. He said it would only make things worse. So having never been in a court situation before in my life I sort of trusted my attorney. So I had to stand there and listen to all their lies. At the end the judge turned to the prosecuting attorney and said" are we still good to go? "The prosecuting attorney said "I think so your honor"

At that point the judge turned to me, and said and I quote "I ASSUME YOU DID THIS?" Almost everybody in the courtroom thought WHAT! It was obvious that the judge, and the court didn't have any idea if the allegations were true or not. That's because there was no crime, and without a crime there can be no evidence. This was all made up, but they proceeded anyway. You see it is hard to get them to see the truth, and know the honest thing to do when they look the other way. It's like talking to a brick wall. Especially after the news media gets involved. I'm sure if you could look at the history of the news media and what they have done to this country I really believe they would be drummed out of business.

Chapter 11

CHECKING IN AT THE FRONT DESK

After I was taken into custody in the court, they took me down on the elevator to the check in area. I was in this area that I had to exchange my civilian duds for a more appropriate attire so I would blend in with the locals. This process took almost three hours to accomplish. All my paperwork was done earlier so all they had to do was get my clothes changed and assign a room. This process should of taken about thirty minutes. However!

I was assigned a suite in one corner of the great 10 foot x 30 foot room that had 17 smaller suites off the main wall, On the other side of the wall was all glass. It was very obvious the county had spent a "lot" of money on this place.

The shower was at one end, and constructed of cement block, and just enough room to turn around in. The inside walls were covered with black mould up and down the inside. You had to push a button to activate the shower water, and no hot or cold just in between somewhere.

The water only lasted about two minutes then you would have to push it again to finish. Such a deal. The rooms were 8 feet wide by 10 feet deep with the ceiling about 12 feet high. No windows only a 12"x12" look out through the door. All concrete except the metal door. Such a nice place to be. The paint was a custom job done by the previous tenants. It seems they all contributed to the decor. This would be a very good place to stay away from however the walls made interesting reading.

Chapter 12

When I first got to the cell there was about 25 inmates there. One of the guards made a point to get right into my face, and yell at me just for ducks. They like to get up close, and personal with all their guests. It must make them feel all warm and fuzzy inside. They try to get you all riled up so you will make a mistake, and yell back at them, or get so mad that you would like to knock their block off. That's what they are good at, and that's what they want. A reason to harass you, and take you to their next step.

The guards try everything they know to get a person to hit them. They take you to the limit. I have never been in jail before, but if it hadn't been for my military experience, the guards actions would have been very disturbing to me. However because of my experience I just laughed at it all. And that made them mad, but again very interesting and funny. The tables were turned on them, and they didn't quite know how to deal with it.

It is very hard to file a complaint simply because all complaints have to go through the guards first, and it's their responsibility to see that its forwarded to the rightful person. Guess what? That never happens. They all cover each others butt, and of course they don't lie or make up stories. Heh ! Right!

The powers that be assigned me to a room with one person in it, and he was a mental case. "Split personality". He was constantly reading about the devil in the Bible, and other things. Interesting person. He was only 22 years old and not a citizen of the United States. Most of the time it was hard to understand his broken English. On the third day we were cleaning our room. My roommate was mopping the floor, and I was getting some rags to wipe down the desk, and bed when my roommate came unglued about 0430 in the morning. He was using a mop with a wooden handle to mop the floor. He went crazy and slammed the mop onto the metal table in the middle of the room. The mop part broke off the wood handle. He then used it for a spear, and threw it at me. I was about 10 feet away with my back turned to him. He threw the spear, and it hit me in the back just above the right shoulder blade. It caused a puncture wound, and it was bleeding. The guards came in, and got him under control, and then they escorted him out of the area. I asked if I could see a medical doctor to patch up the wound, but my request was not heard, and I got no response from the sheriff's department. I never did get a chance to see a doctor about the wound.

Fortunately one of the other tenants of this wonderful hotel was in the military service at one point in time, and was able to help me. He got it all cleaned up, got the blood off, and placed a damp wash cloth over it until it stopped bleeding. The sheriff's department never did come in and ask how I was, and they didn't even take a report.

When the guard that came in that was involved with the incident, I asked him if he reported it, and he said he didn't because they would ask questions, and he didn't want the incident on his record for his shift. He said I looked OK to him, and he quickly dismissed it and left the room.

For the next couple of days I was the only person in my room, and boy was that nice however not long lived.

The next guy they brought in was a tall, and a somewhat dirty person with long unkept hair, and needed a shower very bad. He also had an open bullet wound in his stomach. He had a gauze bandage taped over it, and the guards refused him any medical treatment at that time. I was warned about this guy by some of the other inmates that were there that knew him. They said he was a very unfriendly, and violent person, and he was in for possession of drugs. He was laying in the upper bunk, cussing, and moaning holding his stomach.

I learned a long time ago that the way to defuse a situation like this is to be friendly up front, and try to find out what we had in common if anything. So I went over to talk to him, and introduce myself. The others were right he wasn't the friendliest person I've ever met. After a few minutes talking to him I found out that we had a lot in common, and during the next two weeks became good friends. He had his reasons for being mad at the sheriff's department, and I can't say I blamed him.

He was arrested for possession of a controlled substance. (marijuana). In actuality he had a doctor's prescription for the marijuana which made it legal in all counties, except the one he was arrested in. The only county in the state that does not allow a doctor's note. Go figure! He told the deputy sheriff the situation, and they arrested him anyway.

Two days after he became a guest of the county, his garage was broken into, and his two Harley's were stolen along with a lot of tools. He was not a happy person at this time. He never told me how he got the bullet wound, but it didn't take much to guess.

I found out the he served in the Navy and was assigned to reconnaissance around the same time I was in the Navy. It seems we chewed some of the same dirt so to speak. The sheriff's department was mean, and unkind to him. When food was served they only gave him about half of what everybody else got. So I, and others shared our meals with him.

The sheriff's department made a big stink about it but so what. They couldn't do anything about it. They didn't take care of him so it was up to the rest of us to chip in. When you see the way the sheriff's department treats everybody there is no wonder why we have so many criminals that hate law enforcement, and the judicial system. They create criminals, they don't try to help them or understand them in any way. And that is sad!

Chapter 13

Food not to be taken internally!

The food that was served in jail was not fit for human consumption, and should never be taken internally. Sometimes you were served food you couldn't identify, and it didn't smell good at all. Now this is no joke. Some of the things we were served were not identifiable by smell, or looks. So most of the people didn't eat it, it just went into the trash can. Again, your tax dollars being wasted.

The guards were supposed to eat the same food as we did. However that never happened. They always got good food to eat, and not the stuff they fed us. To give you some kind of idea what the jail food was like, I was there for 30 days, and lost 24 pounds. How's that for a diet?

Here are some examples of what we were given:

Breakfast—Hot cereal that was cold, and runny, and tasted like water—dry rice crispies or dry cherrieos, a small piece of cake—small portion of caned fruit, dry toast and sometimes a boiled egg, and that was sometimes rotten? sometimes warm and sometimes cold milk, but always past the due date. I learned later the milk items were left over from schools that weren't used. They served other things, but my conscience mind has chosen to forget.

Lunch—Peanut butter and jelly sandwich but the peanut butter and jelly are mixed together, and they put it on bread using a ice cream scoop in a ball—a couple pieces of carrots, and celery. To give you variety they would give us a bologna sandwich at least that is what they called it. A very thin piece of meat on dry bread. You also got a small package of kool-aid you could mix with the poor quality water in your sink. That's the only water you could have. I'm trusting I don't have to tell you how it tasted !!! Oh I forgot the best thing. Once in a while they would serve us vegetable soup for lunch. It looked like it would have been good the first time down . . . . but now ?

Dinner: For dinner: They fed us a variety of things for dinner. Most were fairly ok. If you couldn't identify it, and it smelled half way decent you could give it a try. The best they had was a macaroni and cheese dish with hot dogs, and a piece of dry toast, some canned green beans and who knows what else Oh, and applesauce for desert. Boy I'll bet your mouth is just watering by now.

You know what bugs me is the fact that I was told that the DOC receives $150.00 per day per inmate for their care. I found out from the guards that the meals cost only $0.63 cents per serving. So that's about $1.89 per day per person. So where is the other $148.11 per day going? It certainly doesn't go to the maintenance, and up keep of the facility nor does it go to the interior decorator. And I'm sure it doesn't go to the quality of the supervision they provide.

The place is an absolute mess. Without describing the other guests that reside there, I will let your mind wonder about all the creepy, crawly inhabitants that call this wonderful place home. At night some of the guards have races with the food carts down the halls. That's $1,036.77 per person per week and $4,147.08 per person per month! Times all the inmates that call this place home. So tell me why don't the inmates have better food, and living conditions? Its my understanding that one of the local prisons have at least 20% of their inmates sleeping on the cement floor! What's that all about! That's just cruel, and unusual punishment. The sheriff's department jailers don't need to do that. The sheriff's department says they have budget cuts to consider.

My room mate was a diabetic but the sheriff's department would not give him his medication. During one night he started having a seizure in the upper bunk, and flopping around. I got up and realized what was happening. I pushed the intercom, and stated I had a medical emergency, and to get some medical help as soon as they could, but nobody responded. I had to hold him down to keep him from falling to the floor. I managed to get some sweets in him, and he finely calmed down.

I called on the intercom many times to get help but no answer. The next day I told our "house mouse" (that's a person that oversees everything, and has the guard's ear. Or you could call him a snitch!) about the incident, and he quickly reported it to the person in charge. To my knowledge nothing ever became of it. Later on I was transferred to a work release area. One of the nicer guards made a special effort to come over, and tell me that unofficially the sheriff's department was grateful for what I did, and they credit me for saving my roommate's life that night.

Chapter 14

What about the Guards?

One night while in the jail side, I was up late reading using the light coming through the 12"x12" window in my cell. I noticed several guards huddled next to the desk in the open area. Where I was located I could see their computer through the reflection in the window across from my room. They were all watching a porn movie on the internet, and laughing and making comments. I found out that this happens quite often, and has become a regular activity for these guys.

One of the inmates complained to the chaplain that was visiting about the guards' activities, and he in turn mentioned it to the person in charge of the sheriff's department in the jail. I heard that the person in charge just came down, and told the guards not to do that anymore, and that they were using the states computer illegally, and for their own personal use, and entertainment, and they could be terminated for it.

It didn't seem to make any difference they just continued, and that's how things are handled at the jail with the sheriff's department. Sweep everything under the rug, and "don't bother me" type of attitude.

The trouble with the sheriff's department is they do not answer to anyone including the judges. No one in the sheriff's department jail takes responsibility for anything. Once your case leaves the court room the judge doesn't want anything to do with it. The judges can do something if they wanted to, but they don't. The only person that can help is the States Attorney General, or the Governor, but they generally don't want to be bothered ether. If you file a complaint to the jail you have to have all kinds of evidence and witnesses, and that is nearly impossible. Therefore your report lands on deaf ears, and it gets filed in the circular file for future reference. In other words you are screwed until further notice. No voice. Again!

It is very hard to find anyone that cares about you. They are all concerned about themselves. So the sheriff's department jailers continue to do just what they want, and how they want. The general public never knows what happens with the sheriff's department jailers, and they don't want to know.

If the public ever found out how our detainees are treated I think that most people would be absolutely appalled, and request that changes be made. Most people are generally good people, and I think they would call for a grand jury to clean out all the riff raft, wrong doing, and mistreatment of detainees. Then demand a change in the sheriff's department jailer policies, and the way they do things. And believe me there is a lot in the sheriff's department that needs to be changed!

They more then likely would fire most of the employees starting with the people on top. In this case the corruption starts at the top, and runs down hill! They are good at this because it doesn't take any kind of intelligence to be stupid and uncaring. There needs to be a committee or organisation that the sheriff's department jailers answers to. An organisation made up of people like you, to monitor all activities of the jail. An organisation that they have to answer to and an organisation where the inmates, and the parents can go to to be heard. Right now some of the younger kids are not represented at all, and at the present time they have no place to go. Even their parents have no recourse. You say, what about their lawyers? Well let me tell you about that. If you have a court appointed lawyer you,re finished because those lawyers may get to you in about 6 to 9 months after you're put in jail. Again they really don't care, and their case loads are too large to be handled efficiently

When I got into jail there was a man there that was about 71 years old, and had no idea why he was there. He had a court appointed lawyer, and was not visited by him the whole time I was there. The others said he was there for 7 months already, and still no lawyer had talked to him yet. Question: What happened to a persons constitutional right to a speedy trial. When I left he still had not been contacted! WHY?

This doesn't sound like the United States I fought for in the military.

This is not the United States I thought I knew!

Chapter 15

Hiring a Lawyer

If you can afford a lawyer be careful, because they are all officers of the court, and in "cahoots" with each other.

During the year or so I was in their so called county supervision program, I had many court appearances, and for the most part it looked like old home week with the good old' boys club. The judge trying to conduct business, and all the other lawyers, around 15 or so are talking about their families, and what they did during the last weekend. What a joke! You have to remember all these lawyers work in the same county, and they have to get along, and play nice with all the other lawyers so no one make waves for the other. They are all buddy buddy with each other.

Case in point. My case. No evidence, 32 pages of facts, and precedents supporting the fact that I couldn't have committed any crime. But I still went to jail for something I didn't do. So my note to the general public is "Look Out, and Watch Your Back!" Law enforcement these days are so judgemental about everything, and they don't believe the truth. Simply because it is easier to believe a lie then it is to believe the truth. If law enforcement even thinks you may be guilty of a crime they will put you, or your loved ones in jail until they can create some evidence that support their side, and position.

In the Miranda rights they are supposed to read to you, it says "You have the right to be silent, anything you say can and may be held against you in a court of law. You have the right to an attorney, if you cannot afford an attorney one will be appointed to you before any questions". In my case I was never read my rights, and there was several sessions of questioning in regards to the alleged crime I was supposed to have committed.

They questioned me over the phone without my permission, and from third parties acting in behalf of law enforcement doing the investigating. Pretty sneaky, and very illegal especially when they were planning to use it in a court of law. The judge should never have allowed it. When the judge allowed this to happen he became an accomplice to the violation of the law. The judge should go to jail along with the investigative team.

Chapter 16

Can't Trust Anybody

Always remember that all the lawyers and attorneys have been made officers of the court. When you tell them something in confidence they have to by law inform the court of this information. You are screwed! Don't trust anybody! And remember the least said is the easiest mended. Be very careful of what you say because those attorneys, and law enforcement people can take what you said, and turn it around to meet their needs! And absolutely don't trust a psychologist by any means.

These people try to earn your confidence, and trust by telling you they will not say anything because, they have a privacy rule, and they have to honour the therapist client relationship. That is a hole bunch of bologna!! They also have been made officers of the court, and have to by law report anything they encounter that may be classified as a crime by any means. They report directly to the prosecuting attorney. And when they report they will write up their report based on their so called professional opinion. They say something like "according to the average response it is my opinion that this person may be a problem to the general public because Mr XYZ states in his paper on" . . . It goes on and on with their so called opinion, and never addressing your actual problem, if in fact you even have a problem. They make no effort to find out the truth. Its like they have blinders on, and don't want to hear anything other then what the court says.

Like the X-Files the truth is out there!

They just don't want to know about it.

There is no privacy laws in force. All information has to be revealed.

It has been my experience that the only person you can trust or talk to is a person of the church. Your Minister, Father, Preacher or however you would like to identify them. Simply put . . . . nobody owns a church!

Chapter 17

DEPARTMENT OF CORRECTIONS

The year of anguish

After my release from jail **I** was placed in the wonderful care of the Department of Corrections for our county. Boy what a joke! For the most part those people just don't care. They are taken care of, and receive a pay check every month, and it's easy for them. They at this stage just don't have the time or the interest in helping people.

I was instructed to report to DOC within 24 hours of my release from jail. I tried to contact them within the 24 hour period, but the person I was to report to was in some sort of a class for another week or so. So my wife and I sat there in the DOC office for about 45 minutes while the person behind the desk filled out 11 fields on her computer. This is a process that would take the average person with no knowledge of typing about 5 minutes to complete, using the hunt and peck method. Not too much intelligence needed to complete this task. However we are talking about the Department of Corrections run by the state. So why should they try to be efficient when they get paid whether they do the job or not.

About a week or so later I finely checked in with the person I was assigned to, and for all practical purposes let's call him Mr. Sunshine. He didn't just carry a chip on his shoulder he carried the whole box!

I had to report on the first and third Wednesday of every month. I had to fill out a long form every time I reported. Sometimes the report process would take about 15 minutes, and sometimes it would take a couple of hours, depending on how Mr Sunshine felt that day. He, and his side kick, would sit back in the back room and play games on their computer. There would be several people reporting at these times, but Mr. Sunshine was very laid back, and in no hurry to help anybody. In fact in some cases I think he resented being there.

Chapter 18

Home Inspections

The DOC officers would come out to my home and check on me every once in a while. When Mr. Sunshine came out he would always sneak up to the house, and look in the windows before he would knock on the door. There were several times he would scare my kids by looking in the windows. He was just that kind of a person very sneaky and someone not to be trusted.

One time he, and his team, came speeding down our driveway, and almost ran over my wife, and daughter on their bikes. Our driveway is about 200 feet long, and winding through the trees. If you drive slow as you are supposed to, it is safe, but if you are speeding you can run over one of our cats, little animals, and anybody that is on the driveway. Look out!

These guys were driving way too fast for the driveway, and jeopardised the safety of my wife and daughter who were coming back from getting the mail. I brought this to the attention to Mr Sunshine, and he said they were not speeding, and they had it on the video tape in their car to prove it. The truth of the matter is there is no video camera in their car so how do they have a tape? Another bold lie told by Mr. Sunshine, and the DOC.

One of the times they came over I was outside sitting on the front porch reading a book. Our front porch runs along one side, across the front of the house, and down the other side. Anyway while sitting there they came up to the house, and started looking in the windows.

They didn't see me quietly sitting there. As they came over to the office window where I was sitting they put their hands up to the glass to look in, and I couldn't resist the temptation. With a nice strong voice, and fairly loud I said "CAN I HELP YOU!!!" Scared the crap out of Mr Sunshine, and he got very upset accusing me of sneaking up on him. Even though I was just sitting there. He was so intent in looking into my home he didn't even see me sitting there about 8 feet away.

About 3 months before my supervision was over, the state in their infinite wisdom decided to let these questionable people carry a concealed weapon, and arm themselves. Why? Not sure! That was a dangerous joke in the making. About three weeks after they all received their permits to carry a gun, Mr. Sunshine was on a home inspection, and for what ever reason he decided to draw his weapon to, I guess, assert his authority, He ended up dropping it on his foot. The person he was supervising picked up his weapon, and gave it back to him.

Boy what efficiency! These guys are an accident looking for a place to happen. Heaven help us if they ever get into a situation where they really needed to use it, If they had to fire it . . . . could they hit the side of a barn while standing on the inside? This story was told to the group while waiting for . . . . you guessed it, Mr Sunshine. Judging from all the other things I've seen from these people I think the best place, and most safe place to be while they are shooting their gun, is right in front of them.

While in the wonderful care of DOC you are required to take a UA (urine analysis) at least once a month, I guess to check if your are drinking, or taking drugs. I have never done either, but it didn't make any difference. You had to go into the restroom, which is in the lobby, and pee in a small jar, These guys make a big deal of watching you pee. They have to see the whole process. I guess to make sure you are not cheating, or something. Is that possible? If you couldn't pee they gave you about an hour to fill your bladder, and if you still couldn't do it they considered you as going against the judge's orders, They place you under arrest, and put you in jail awaiting a court hearing. But there is no pressure! It is all part of the wonderful experience!

Along with all these niceties, you were required to take, and pass, a polygraph every 3 months. Passing the polygraph is required if you ever want to get past the county supervision, and get off their grid. It is required by the court. What a joke because the polygraph can be changed, and manipulated, during the questioning. That would be the main reason the court doesn't allow the polygraph in court as evidence anymore. It is not reliable, and the operator can easily fake the results.

In talking to the other guests they always have you fail the first polygraph. (That's a given.) That seems to be standard procedure. When you fail the first polygraph the DOC can make it really hard on you during your reporting process.

About a couple of weeks had passed since I failed the first polygraph. So DOC sent a team out to inspect my home. They had absolutely no reason, cause, or right to do that. I think they just wanted to impress my family, and let them know that they are in charge, and we couldn't do anything about it. That was the feeling they presented.

They sat me down on the couch, and made my two daughters go out to the garage, and sit in the car. The six of them proceeded to ransack my home, and shop area. They opened drawers, opened and looked into boxes, opened closets, and basically got into everything in the house, my office, and shop area.

At one time Mr Sunshine was in my office, and my wife went in to see what he was doing, and he made the comment for her to get out, and sit on the couch with me. Now according to the law, my wife had every right to monitor what he was doing, but he didn't see it that way. Because there is no governing body, group, or committee to file a complaint with, just who would my wife complain to. These people knew that.

I keep a safe on my desk. It has never been locked in the whole time it's been there. However Mr Sunshine in his wisdom was fiddling around with the knob on the front, and instead of just opening the door he ended up locking it. Then he got mad because I at that time couldn't remember the combination. I never lock the thing, and I got it about three years earlier. He wanted to know if I was hiding anything in there. I place important things in there just so I can keep track of where they are. I finely remembered the combination, and he opened the safe, then proceeded to take everything out. When putting things back he dropped some things on the floor, but didn't pick them up.

Later when I went in to clean everything up, and get things organised again, I found several items on the floor. So I decided to take inventory of the remaining items in the safe. I had a wooden box with some gold dollars in it $50.00 to be exact. The top was off the box, and there were about $15.00 missing. The coins were there when he started but, missing when he was finished. Now it doesn't take a rocked scientist to figure out what happened. I sometimes wonder how many things walk away when he is through with the different home searches.

The DOC rules clearly state the home search shall be a visual inspection only, and this inspection is limited to where the person in question frequents, and not the entire home. So again DOC has broken the law. He cannot open drawers, look into closets, open cupboards, and especially remove articles from any safe.

My family received a round tin of Christmas cookies that hadn't been opened yet. It sat by my desk. My wife said that Mr Sunshine was trying to get it open, and couldn't. She said it was one of the funniest things she has seen in a long time . . . watching this guy trying to get into this tin of cookies. It was sealed with cellophane packing tape from the factory, and apparently DOC proof, because this guy never did get it open. How's that for intelligence!

You know, it is very sad that DOC is the way they are but you have to look on the bright side of things they do provide a source of entertainment for many people under their care.

Chapter 19

Miscellaneous Information

IN JAIL

Phone:

Most jails are arranged so that people can phone out and make collect calls. Sadly, we discovered after two days waiting for a call, that although that works in some cases it does not work in all. We live in a small city with it's own phone company. The jail did not have an agreement with this company, so no collect calls were allowed. Instead, we needed to go to Walmart, and deposit funds in a special account which then could be accessed by the phone in the jail.

Note, call the jail immediately if you do not receive a call from your loved one. There may extra steps required to allow them to call out.

Additionally, there are often very few phones in ratio to the number of prisoners in the jail. My husband shared two phones among thirty eight people, and one of the two phones had very poor reception. So, you will need to be patient sometimes, because they just don't get a chance to make a phone call every day.

Books/Reading Material

The jail will allow people to have reading materials. They have some semblance of a "library" which consists of trashed paperbacks, usually missing several pages. So, the best way to handle this is to order books on line from Amazon, Barnes and Noble, Borders Books, etc. and have them sent directly to your loved one in the jail. This is also the fastest way in most cases to get books to your loved one.

Money for Snacks and necessities:

It is very necessary for your family to put money on an account so you can order against it. Things like, candy bars, snack foods, paper, envelopes, pencils, clothing, shorts, shirts, socks, tooth paste, tooth brush, and many other things that are needed. The jail gives you a couple of things to start with but after that you have to purchase everything else. You need to maintain an account, and what you really need to do is track your account because it can get off real fast. Keep all your receipts!! If they don't have the item you ordered they will substitute something else, and you can count on it not being the same price but higher.

Once a person ordered 10 envelopes and he received 400, Mistake? Yes ! Did he have to pay for them, you bet. They just deducted it off his account, and brought his balance almost to zero, give or take a couple of pennies. I saw a lot of honor and respect among the prisoners. When this happened at first it was kind of comical but you have to admit very stupid with a capitol "S" Anyway any person that needed envelopes went to this guy and he would let them have the amount they needed. In return the ones that borrowed the envelopes would let this person order what he needed off the persons account, and that's how payment was made to compensate for the envelopes. It all worked out just fine, and everybody was happy except of course the guards. They frowned on this kind of activity they said it screwed up their books and it wasn't allowed. And of course like everything else it didn't make sense to anyone except the guards. O course they were ignored as usual.

The Guards:

Boy what can be said for these wonderful people that express so much understanding and compassion towards all the guests in this wonderful, and exciting all expense paid county vacation resort. You are the guest of the county, and they see to it that all your needs are barely met. Other than a stainless steel toilet, and a very small sink with only one water faucet, and two beds that attach to the wall with chains on ether end. The beds are made of steel and have a mattress only 1/2 thick, two sheets one large and one small, no pillow, a small steel desk no drawers, and only one chair for two people and sometimes 3 to 4 people are assigned to the room depending on how much money the county wants to make. Yes there is barely enough room in this 8'x10' room for two, but yes they sometimes put 4 people in this little room with the two extra sleeping on the floor. One had to straddle the toilet so all could fit in. If I hadn't seen and experienced this on my own I wouldn't have believed it. And like I said before at least half of the people are there by mistake. The prosecutors and the courts need to do it right, but they say budget cuts prevent them from a formal investigation. So a lot of the evidence falls into the cracks, and you fall into jail erroneously.

Medication:

If you are under a doctor's care you need to bring in all your medication along with the doctor's orders. I need to point out here that even though you bring in your own medication the DOC doesn't have to give it to you. In my case I have to take two daily pills in the morning. I didn't get them for two days. Then when I did get them they were replaced by generic pills and not the original. My pills have a number stamped on the pill itself, but the ones they gave me did not. When I asked the nurse she said they replaced my pills because it was cheaper. I told her I brought my own medication with me, and if I didn't get them the next morning I would be in contact with my attorney, and doctor. After a day they did give me my original medication back. But you have to keep on top of them.

You have to watch everything you do while in jail. You have to be very careful. Anytime you order something or request to go and see the doctor you have to pay for it. The doctor is in the office only 2 days a week. One of the other guests of this wonderful facility wanted to see the doctor for a headache. The guards took him down, and they were gone about 20 minutes. He came back with 2 aspirins. That doesn't seem to be uncommon but what is uncommon is they charged him $70.00 for the two aspirin. You should have heard him complain. And then the public wonders why these people get mad at the Sheriff's department who runs the jail. They take advantage any way they can. When I was first checked into the the jail they went through my wallet, and took out all my money. They kept $100.00 for themselves. This was called a booking fee, and was standard procedure at that time. About a year, and many complaints later the county finely determined it was illegal to steal a persons money like that, and put a stop to it. I don't see any refunds!!!

Visitors:

Consult the handouts carefully which tell about your visitation rights. Generally visitation is allowed twice a week for two people on each occasion. However, the two people should attend the visitation together . . . . because each inmate only gets to come out once each day to see visitors. Also, be careful what is said. There are signs everywhere saying that the conversations are recorded.

Documents:

If you have need to have business or personal documents signed the best way is to have a lawyer go to the jail for signatures. I tried to have a Power of Attorney signed while I was in jail but it turned out looking like a first grader did it. It was awful. I had it turned it in at the front desk and it was "lost" for approximately three days. When it was returned it looked like a truck had driven over it, there were "scratch outs" by the one witnessing my signature, and it looked terrible. I would have been embarrassed to turn it in too anyone.

Then I asked a lawyer to take charge and have the document signed, which was done immediately, and it looked like a normal document. Of course, this turned out to be very pricey (upward of one thousand dollars).

They must have made the lawyer wait a couple hours before allowing him in to have the document signed. Since only three signatures were required on a three page document that equates to about $350 per page. At least it was legible, and my wife was able to use it in closing the sale of a home that we had built.

Mail:

All mail is opened, and read before you receive it. They go through everything. People from the outside can send you mail but letters only. No books or anything else unless it is ordered and sent from a book store or a known publisher, or company. All else is taken, and you don't know anything about it. They keep it to themselves.

Code of ethics among prisoners:

There is a definite code of ethics among the detainees. I found out they all support one another in many different ways. They have to stick together because the guards seem to take the position of putting themselves on a pedestal looking down on everybody. They view themselves as the good guys having never done anything against the law in their life. You however are bad, and corrupt but they don't know why, and in most cases what you are in for. They know you are bad for everybody. And that is all they want to know. No effort is made to find out about you or how they can help.

The guards try their best to make it tough on as many people as they can. They get right in you face and yell at you, and try to get you aggravated so you may loose your temper, and do something stupid. And that's what they are waiting for. You see they are not in the public view, they are by themselves with others like them to support their actions no matter how wrong it is, and they all stick together. If you do loose your

temper and even act like you are going to strike the guard they throw
you on the floor, slap hand cuffs on you, and take you to what they so
laughingly call the hole.

The hole is a very tiny room with one steel bunk a little sink, and a
stainless toilet. You are not allowed anything else. No letter writing, no
reading a book, you just have to sit there. You could be in there anywhere
from one day up to five days or more depending on how the guard feels.
There are no rules of how long, it just depends on how the guard feels.

To give you a better idea of how their thinking is, there was a
gentleman that was in jail when I got there. He was over 71 years old,
and basically had no idea why he was there. Nobody would tell him why?
The guards put him in a room by himself simply because he didn't have
control of all of his body functions. He was on medication, but unless
another inmate got him to the door to receive it he didn't get it, and of
course the nurse wouldn't give the medication to anyone else except the
person they are intended for, and they refused to come into the room.
You see the guards would not go to his room, and advise this gentleman
that the nurse was there. They held to the fact it was his responsibility to
be at the door when medication was handed out, and if he wasn't there
they looked at it as him refusing to take his medicine, and entered it into
the shift log that way.

When the nurse came to the door it was about 0430 in the morning,
and she was only there long enough to give out the medication, and that
was it. You couldn't call her back. She told everybody there she had more
important things to do.

This 71 year old person would have trouble remembering to show
up for chow. The inmates again stepped up to the plate, and assisted
in helping him get his meals, and medication. Of course based on the
quality of the food I'm not sure they did him any favours.

The food in the jail didn't agree with him so most of the time he
spent some money ordering snacks, candy, and crackers from the jail
store.

One day this gentlemen soiled his clothes, and it was really necessary
that he have some assistance, and needed someone to clean him up.
When one of the inmates got the attention of one of the guards, and told
him the problem he would not respond. He said it was not his problem
or responsibility, and they couldn't do anything about it. A couple of the
inmates started cleaning him up, and it was obvious he needed clean
clothes, and the ones he had on should be burned. The guard took
about an hour to round up clean clothes for this guy. Even though the
laundry room was just across the hall from us. All the guards had to do
is walk across the hall, and take the clean clothes off the shelf. But that

seemed too hard for them to do. When the guard finally got the clothes he opened the main door, and just threw the clothes in on the floor and left.

That's our wonderful tax dollars at work.

Inmates are people too. They bleed, feel pain, laugh, love, have compassion for others, and all the other things you do. People are in jail, and prison for basically three reasons. One is because they have been falsely accused of something they didn't do, and the investigating personal didn't do a very good job researching the case. Secondly, they did do something wrong, but very minor. The best correction for this situation would be for a judge to say look, what you did was wrong, but if give me your word, and your promise not to repeat this offence again the court will be lenient with you, and let you go, but I don't want to see you in court again. This treatment would be enough to correct any future actions with his person, and many others because people are generally good people. Sometimes we all need a second chance to make good. Unfortunately our judicial system wants to put as many people in jail as they can because of the money issue.

Then you have the third type of person that could be a problem to other people. But the courts need to rely on hard physical, and factual evidence in these cases. Evidence where there is no question as to the guilt of the person. Do not use the testimony or tapes or any kind of electronic recordings, hear say, or circumstantial evidence. You don't want to use anything that can be changed, or forged in any way, shape, or form. In this day, and age our computers can change almost anything. Sometimes even an eye witness will lie about what they saw. Again the court needs to use hard physical evidence that can't be changed. That's the only thing they should use to convict a person!

Take a good look at the movie industry. With their equipment they can generate anything they want in order to make you believe any kind of story or situation. Remember the eye sees what it wants to see, and your brain thinks what it wants to think based on all the data you have stored in it in the past years, and how you were brought up as a child, your experiences., and ability to understand without emotional interference.

Special note: When you get up in court to testify you have to take an oath on honesty. Wouldn't it be nice if all the attorneys would have to take the same oath.

Chapter 20

THE LOCAL HEAD SHRINK

At the "Pre Sentencing Investigation", (PSI) I was ordered by the Judge to undergo a sexual psychological exam to see if I would be a danger to the public or not. The psychologist I was ordered to see was about 62 miles from my home. I scheduled an appointment, and my wife and I drove up to see this psychologist. At that time I took four (4) polygraph exams, answered three (3) hours of their questions, and an oral exam etc. The exam was about 8 hours in length. We went thorough a lot of questionnaires, and personal interviews with my wife and I.

The first thing they did was a short interview with the person in charge. He told me that everything I said or discussed with him or his staff was in complete confidence, and private. He said by law, and their privacy policy, they couldn't say anything without my written approval. So we had a short talk about things that happened, and didn't happen, and my opinion. I made sure this person knew up front that I did not commit any crime, and have always maintained my innocence in this case. I had to go into another room to take a written test.

While I was in the other room the head person called my wife into his office, and started talking to her about me. My chair was still warm, and the owner was telling my wife everything we talked about. No confidence what so ever, and no privacy policy at all. What happened to the privacy rules? I guess that was just for conversation, and not reality.

At that time he told my wife everything he, and I talked about, and then some. What happened to their privacy policy? I didn't have anything to hide, and my wife knew about everything that was happening anyway. The first thing this person did is start telling a lie right off the bat. How does that make me feel? My wife was very surprised, and disappointed at the actions of the person in charge, and there so called "privacy policy". I knew, from that time on I couldn't trust them for a second. "Don't trust anybody!"

When a person gets involved with this kind of situation, and starts talking to a sexual psychologist you have to wonder, and ask yourself why did this person want to get involved in this kind of work in the first place. Did he or she go through something like this in their life that sparked their interest, or are they turned on by somebody else's sexual situation and troubles. Some people are you know! It seemed to me that the people that I talked to had some kind of sexual problem of their own to deal with. When one of the female therapists started talking about her clients sexual problems, she would get flushed in the face, and start talking fast. It was very obvious she was getting excited with the subject matter. Why is she a therapist and not a client?

For my case the Court needed to have this report done by the 20th of the month, but the head psychologist didn't get it turned in until sometime the following month which was late. I can't help think this was done on purpose. Simply because, he knew from his experience of several years that if he didn't turn it in in time, there wouldn't be enough time to enter it into record, and I would be ordered by the judge to undergo treatment on a continuing basis for the term of the county supervision program. The head psychiatrist would then assign me a therapist, and I would be ordered by the court to pay for this treatment. Forced payment what a deal for them! After interviewing several other people for this book, I found out they were in the same boat that I was. The head person was late with those people too. I am almost positive that if the court wasn't giving this person clients all the time he would be out of business. Simply put . . . . Nobody in his or her right mind would sign up for this kind of mistreatment and hurt!

Regardless of how much it was I would have to pay. I know this because when the head psychiatrist wrote a letter to my community corrections officer he charged me $750.00 for a letter with only two paragraphs in it. I called it to his attention, and I said that sounded like too much to charge for a letter. His receptionist's response was, and I quote "I need to pay the bill or go to jail." I made enough noise to get it down to somewhat lower amount of $500.00, but that is still too much, I was forced by community corrections (DOC), and the court to pay the bill, you guessed it . . . or go to jail.

If it wasn't for the courts, these sexual psychologists would be out of business. No one in their right mind would sign up, and pay for this kind of mental abuse, and nasty treatment. These psychiatrists know just how to play the courts, and are able to charge anything they want, and the court forces the client to pay.

After over 8 hours of polygraph, written exams, and and oral exams the head psychologist arrived at the conclusion that I tested normal, and I didn't qualify for any sexual treatment, and he said he would stand behind his statement. So why did I have to go through all those meetings, and what they laughingly call therapy?

The psychologist knew the system, and he knew if he was late handing in his report about me there wouldn't be enough time for the judge to act on it, and order therapy instead of dismissing it. Again he knew just how to play the court system, and how to get just what he wanted. Again there is nobody to supervise these people, and provide a vehicle for someone to file a complaint with.

I was then scheduled for some private sessions with one of their cracker jack therapists. At the first meeting she talked to me about the alleged offence. She had the final analysis of the test, and polygraph to discuss. She told me the only red flag she could find is about pornography on my computer. The report said that I looked for porn on my computer when in fact I told the examiner that pornography sometimes comes up when I am searching for other things. Example: When my wife and I were searching on the Disney store for Christmas items; while backing out of the web sites some pornography pages came up all by themselves with no help.

Also when my daughter was at the school library looking up some reference material she also experienced pornography sites coming up, and brought it to the attention of her teacher. If you own a computer you automatically have many pornography web sites listed in you cache'. Every PC is a porno sponge whether you know it or not. A lot of companies that support pornography sites are able to send them to all PC computers under your existing program. They do this so they can use your computer to transmit their porno e-mail using your computer, and ID and you don't know anything about it.

One of the very first things that happened to me is when I finished the first session with the therapist for what ever reason she e-mailed Mr. Sunshine and told him that I asked her to breakfast that morning. At my regular check in meeting he read me the riot act and told me I wasn't authorised to ask the therapist for a date, and the next time I did that he would put me in jail. I assured him that was never the case. Why on earth would I do something like that. It would be as bad as asking MR Sunshine to lunch. No way in hell!!

Chapter 21

What is a Therapist?

A therapist is defined as a person giving treatment intended to relieve, treat, or heal a disorder. However I don't think these court appointed psychiatrist are qualified. I don't think any of them have read the definition because during my contact with this person, I have witnessed several occasions where she has caused family problems, hurt the client, and their families in several ways, and continually belittled her clients. She is responsible for hurting several people in my group. This person should never be allowed to council people. She does more harm than good.

After talking to several people I found out later that this therapist was molested, and taken advantage of when she was a child, and that this is her life goal to get back at as many males as she can. I and several other people believe she became a sex therapist so she could work in the field where she can control men when they were assigned to her. She does this out of revenge, and not out of love, or a concern to help people.

The therapist submits a report to the court on the progress of the person in her care. The therapist can keep you there as long as they want. All they have to do is report to the judge that this person needs a little more time, and the judge always grants it. Even though it is not needed. Remember, it's just the opinion of the person doing the testing. It is all guess work at best! And if they guess wrong you and your family pay the price. This is not an exact science, and this is no joke!

One of the young men I talked to was there for four years going through this so called treatment. During one of the meetings the therapist told him that she thinks they should keep him another year or so until they felt he was OK to enter the public again. The fact of the matter is he was convicted of a misdemeanour, and released with no jail time. The court suggested he sign up for therapy meetings. But yet after a couple of meetings the therapist suggested to the judge they keep him there until they felt he would not hurt anyone. He didn't hurt anyone in the first place. So why are they keeping him longer? The answer is money! These psychiatrist people really have a racket going. They are all part of the judicial net that is so corrupt, and one sided.

In my case after taking over 8 hours of testing along with several polygraphs' it was determined that I didn't need any therapy nor did I need any counselling. I didn't qualify for their treatments. I was OK, and normal as you. But when I met the therapist, she decided to keep me for the rest of the year for evaluation at my expense. That's how these people make their money. If it wasn't for the courts making people attend these meetings and forcing them to pay, the therapist would not make any money at all. Who would drive 62 miles to be put down, ridiculed, and then pay $100.00 for the monthly meeting. And the kicker with this; if you don't pay the therapist she calls the judge, and DOC puts you in jail for not following the courts orders. Again there is no agency or committee or anyone to report this too . . . no one to listen. These people know this, and they keep going, and going, and going . . . .

Chapter 22

No Contact Order

As part of the sentencing agreement I was given a no contact order in reference to the young girl that I allegedly assaulted. That makes sense, and I certainly had no desire to see her again anyway.

About two years after the sentencing I was served with a subpoena to appear in court. The mother of the girl wanted a "no contact order" for herself and her other daughter. It turns out the older daughter had moved out of the home. Now the mother has no recourse to prevent me from contacting her for what ever reason. The no contact order was against the older daughter and now she is gone.

The mother wants a no contact order to be granted to her younger daughter so if she sees me in a store she can call the sheriffs department to come and arrest me for violating the new order. The mother always comes up with something new.

The mother always brings all her paperwork about past experiences, and proceeds to tell the judge everything right from the start every time. She said she saw me at a local establishment, and thought I was looking at her younger daughter (not the one involved in the original accusation), and contemplating some sort of crime. The fact of the mater was, I and my family were sitting at the table having something to eat, and none of us saw the mother or her daughter, ever! So she calls the sheriff to come, and arrest me for what she thought I was thinking.

Here is the surprise! The judge issued a temporary no contact order because of what she thought I was thinking. Again the judicial system is acting on emotion instead of fact. And the real kicker is, I have only seen the younger daughter about a half dozen times about 9 years earlier, and haven't seen her since. I wouldn't know the younger daughter if she came up to me, and said hi. But yet, the mother was issued a temporary no contact order because she somehow convinced the judge I was thinking about something I shouldn't have. They should make a movie about that!

That shows you how corrupt, and judgemental the courts are. The judges think with their human emotions rather then the letter of the law. The act does not follow the law as far as issuing a no contact order. The order is designed to keep people apart to cool down after an incident. Not to punish people as to what they are or are not thinking, especially after nine years of not seeing the person.

Fortunately, when this came before the judge the permanent restraining order was denied. The judge ruling in this instance was very sane and abided by what one would assume was the actual law.

The News Media

Lets have a talk about the news media. The news media has the right to publication given to them by the Constitution of the United States. They are able to report the news as it is in respect to the truth and honestly with the subject matter at hand. When reporting they should still respect everybody's rights and privacy. They do not have the authority nor the right to degrade, endanger or violate anyone's privacy or anything else because of what they say. They need to write the truth based on fact, and not on what someone has said about another person or place.

Everyone reads the news paper. Be honest now . . . . How many of you believe the things you read? You should only believe 2% of what they print. The rest of the 98% is paper fill, slanted in their direction to make you believe what they want.

How many of you have heard of subliminal messages? Subliminal by definition is a stimulus or mental process below the threshold of sensation or consciousness; perceived by or affecting someone's mind without their being aware of it. They can make you believe anything they want and you wouldn't even know that you were manipulated or in a more common term Brain Washed.

The news media can be a wonderful way to keep up on activities around us. But when they start writing articles the way they want, and not telling the truth, or just telling only one side of the story (and of course that's their side, the side that sells papers) that's when they become very dangerous. They are attempting to get you to believe their way of thinking. A friend of mine once told me a story of a reporter in Viet Nam that invited himself into a mission briefing. He printed the information, and the the other side was waiting for our marines. They were ambushed and seven were killed because of it. When this was brought to their attention they tried to justify their actions, and said quote "the other side had the right to know what we were up to" . . . unquote.

There are reporters in the news media just like that one that caused the deaths of those marines. They are all for getting the story, and getting it first, and the story is all they care about. These reporters couldn't care less about you and me, just the story! They will report, and print anything and in any way they can to sell papers, and retain their job. They will tell a story twisted to the point of character assignation for the person they are writing about. If the reporter writing your story doesn't like you then you are screwed. Then try to get the paper to take it back. Not a chance. They would be admitting they made a mistake, and as we know, they never make mistakes. They do a lot of damage to people, court cases, businesses, schools, colleges, and they do it while standing behind the First Amendment of our Constitution of the United States. Freedom of the press. That doesn't mean that they can take away your freedom while they do that. That's the same Constitution I and many of you fought for in combat.

In court cases they should not be allowed to publish the name of any person until the court has come to a final discussion on the alleged crime. By publishing a person's name they are endangering that person, and effecting the outcome of any fair trial by jury or judge. The news is very opinionated about different subject matters that should be left alone until the termination of the trial, and a final verdict recorded. The publication of any private information can put the alleged person in physical danger from other people that read the news. They like to take things into their own hands, and pat themselves on the back for their actions. Then they hope other people will understand their actions and give them praises, and say we understand. Even in some cases when they are arrested for their actions, the judge will sometimes judge them innocent just because they say they acted out of temporary insanity, and they weren't thinking clearly.

In this case the news media appointed themselves as judge, jury, and executioner for this person. Now after it is over, it is now determined that there was no evidence to support that any crime was ever committed in the first place. So tell me. Just how is the news media going to make right what they did? The answer is they won't. It was a good story when published and they were able to sell a lot of papers because of it. But as for retracting what they said or trying to return my credibility, or honour, not a chance. All they say is sorry, and go on with their miserable unethical existence.

Every freeman has an undoubted right to lay what sentiments he pleases before the public; to forbid this, is to destroy the freedom of the press: but if he publishes what is improper, mischievous, or illegal, he must take the consequences of his own temerity.

(First Amendment of the Constitution of the Untied States of America)

Conclusion

You dear reader are involved with one of the greatest professions or hobbies you could possibly get involved in. The art of creating with light. That's what photography is. The art of painting with light. The creation of your thought, and how you perceive things in you thinking, and how you present it to other people. The photographer is the expression of who he or she is. Your work is the example of your life, and how you see others.

You can create a 1,000 page book with one photograph. You can bring out the softness of the new-born, or the passion of a single human being, or the tenderness of a little kitten. This you can create with your camera, and your inner passion for creation.

But in your quest for your love of photography you must be aware that there are certain people who have a different idea about you, and what you do, and want to take away your ability to make other people happy.

Instead they want to suck out your creational energy to boost themselves up for whatever reason. Some people just feed off others to get some kind of joy out of causing a person grief. It seems to give them some sense of power.

A lot of times they will do anything to accomplish this including degrading a person, lying, telling false stories, and misleading people to fill some kind of void they have. And now they have the ability to say anything they want, and place it on the internet. They don't seem to understand that once a story gets out that's it. It can never be taken back. The damage has been done. They can't seem to do anything on their own, but need the help of others to do this.

If you ever find yourself in this kind of situation please be very careful about what you say and do. Remember the authorities will record everything you say for future reference. They formulate their questions to head you in a specific direction, and they try to put words in your mouth, and get you to say things you don't mean, or say something that can be taken several different ways. Then they can interpret them anyway they want for the investigation, and the court. They can work you, and manoeuvre you like a puppet.

So what it boils down to is this, don't get into this situation in the first place if you can help it. If you ever find yourself in the position where you think you may need the help, and advice of an attorney the main thing you should know is all attorneys are officers of the court reporting to the prosecuting attorney. So they can't be trusted, but you can't do anything without them. To put it into simple terms, the court requires you to be represented by a legal counsel. The courts, and the prosecutors office needs to know what you are up to. They think they need to keep track of what you are doing.

It is in your best interest to try and get an attorney outside of your county or at least outside of the county in which the alleged crime was to of taken place. Every county is like a family. You scratch my back and I will give you inside information on what is happening, and maybe we can make some sort of deal.

If you do get into this kind of a situation use your own judgement, but if I had it to do over again I would not choose an attorney in the same county. Go to a different county for all your legal advice. If you are all in the same county you may not have a chance in beating any case. Remember all the attorneys that are in the same county, are so-to-speak in the same sandbox, and must play nice with each other, and get along. If you feel you need to talk to someone seek out the pastor of your church or the help of an ordained minister of a church. They are obligated to keep everything confidential and private. They don't go blabbing it all over the place like a lawyer, or psychiatrist does. I wouldn't give them time of day, unless I wanted everybody to know.

Please understand it doesn't make any difference whether you are guilty or not, that's not the point. As soon as any accusation is made they want you in jail. Period! And will do anything possible to hold you. (it's the money thing again) Once you get in their radar you are fair game. Unless you hire a good attorney, you are just treading water, and waiting for the sharks to bite you in the . . . .

When talking to an attorney, and you want to maintain your innocence ask him about the "Alford Plea." In the law of the United States an Alford plea is a plea in criminal court in which the defendant does not admit to the act, and asserts his or her innocence, but admits that the court may have some sort of belief of evidence with which the prosecution could likely convince a judge or jury to find the defendant guilty. It is called circumstantial evidence along with human emotion. If they have hard facts, and evidence then they would not allow you to use the Alford Plea. If they believe you may be innocent they will allow the Alford Plea.

As a photographer, the things you need to have is; a good model release, and property release. There are many different kinds, and you can find most of them in photography books, or on the internet. Be sure to get one that pertains to your photography interests, and clients needs. Remember if you can recognise somebody in your photo, you need a model release signed by the model or the person you took a picture of. If you or anybody else can recognise an item, or place you photographed you need to fill out a property release signed by the owner giving you permission to take the photo. Now that's only if you have plans of selling the pictures for money or try to get them published. If somebody can recognise it they want money for it. Unless you have the proper release! If you don't plan on selling the photos don't worry about it.

Be sure you have a contract with all items spelled out about what your roll is, and the roll of your client. What and who the photos are for, and be clear on clothing, props, and poses. What mood, or atmosphere are they trying to generate with the photos, clothing and background.

Keep a detailed resume of all activities about the photo shoot. People that witnessed the shoot, and can collaborate with you as to your conduct during the shoot. Also be sure to list all locations were the photos took place. Male or female, always have a second person there to witness the photo shoot. It may not do any good, but at least it shows that you are attempting to do the right thing.

After going through all the court hearings and judgements it was hard for me to understand why the system went ahead without any evidence. I am not guilty of any crime! I don't understand why that happened. However after going through the system, and spending some time in jail, I now know for a fact that some others have been accused of a similar crime, and convicted without any evidence to back up the allegations.

People that are accused of a crime like this, are automatically looked down on by the majority of the public. They don't want you near them because of what they have read in the news papers, or seen on TV, and not the truth.

If you have never been evolved with the judicial system don't plan on it.

Its Not Fun!

Because of the sheriff's department not doing a complete investigation, I paid for it with thirty days in jail. Now because of this fact, I lost my business, I can't get a any kind of employment with any company. If I didn't already have a home I couldn't even rent an apartment. They all do background checks, and when they find out you have been in jail they automatically don't want your around. It makes life extremely difficult to make ends meet, and put food on the table for your family.

This is especially hard for my family to go through this because they know it is all a lie created in the thinking of the mother. I don't know how she can possibly sleep at night knowing what she has done. How about her daughter? How do you think she is going to respond, and handle destroying a persons family life? Later on in her life she is going to think back on this, and know that no mater what she does she can never make up for her or her mothers actions, and my family's loss. I hope she can cope with it. Having a conscience that will bother her twenty four hours a day is not what I would want. The mother is an evil person and the daughter knows this. The daughter has tried to run away several times but was always brought back.

I hope the daughter gets a copy of this book because I want her to know this. I and my family forgive her for everything that has been done to me and my family in her name. From this day you need to go forward and don't look back. I don't hold you responsible for anything. In order for your healing process to start or become complete you need to forgive yourself as well.

It is all water under the bridge and past. The past is gone and the future is not her yet. You only have right now. Remember today is a new day full of blessings. Treat it as a new slate and go forward. Never hold a grudge against anyone and try to go through your life loving your neighbour as yourself and be merciful just and pure.

www.ingramcontent.com/pod-product-compliance
Lightning Source LLC
Chambersburg PA
CBHW022128170526
45157CB00004B/1792